Where do shadows come from?

why ? why ? why ?

Where do shadows come from?

Rosie Greenwood

p

This is a Parragon Publishing Book
First published in 2001

Parragon Publishing
Queen Street House
4 Queen Street
Bath BA1 1HE, UK

Copyright © Parragon 2001

Produced by

David West 👥 Children's Books
7 Princeton Court
55 Felsham Road
Putney
London SW15 1AZ, UK

British Library Cataloguing-in-Publication Data

A catalogue record for this book is available from
the British Library.

ISBN 0-75256-394-7

Printed in Italy

Designers
Aarti Parmar, Rob Shone, Fiona Thorne

Illustrator
Janie Perie (Allied Artists)

Cartoonist
Peter Wilks (SGA)

Editor
James Pickering

CONTENTS

? What is air made of?

Air is a mixture of invisible gases. The main ones are nitrogen and oxygen, but there's also some carbon dioxide, water vapor and other gases, as well as tiny bits of salt, dust and dirt.

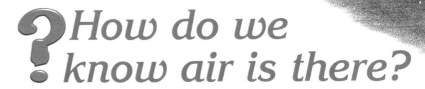

? How do we know air is there?

We can't see or taste or smell air, but we can feel and hear it when the wind blows. Wind is moving air – it's what makes trees bend and leaves rustle, and what blows sailboats across the water.

?Is there air in Space?

The skin of air around the Earth is called the atmosphere, and it fades away into nothingness at about 300 miles above the ground – that's where Space begins. There's no air in Space, but most of the other planets have their own atmospheres.

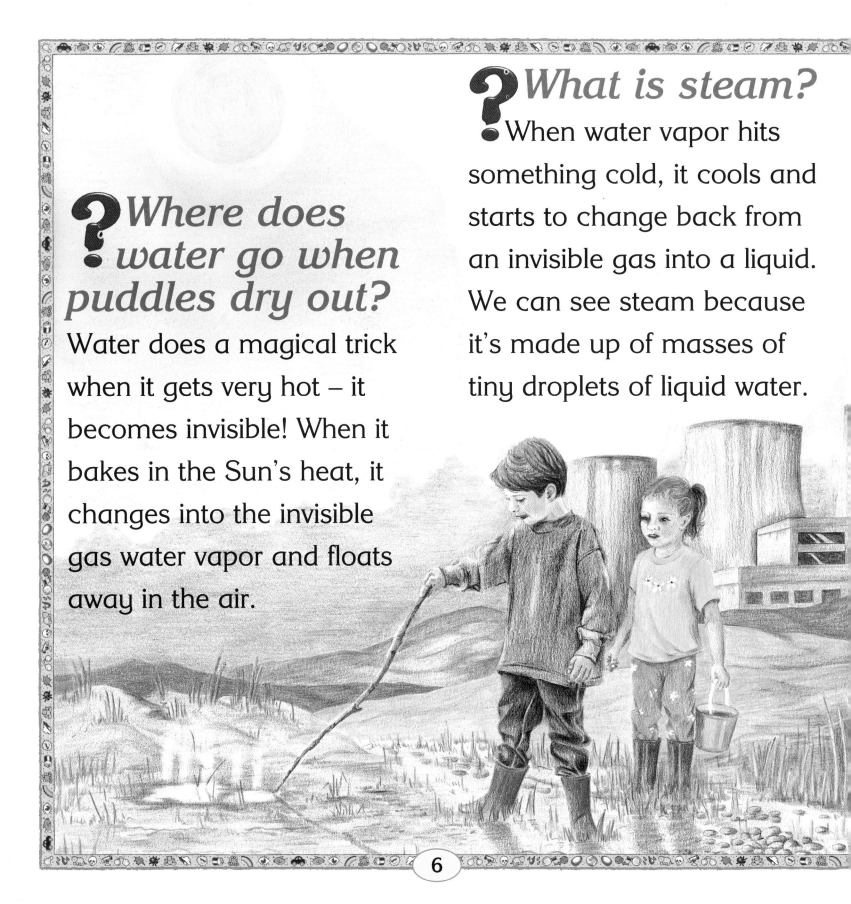

? Where does water go when puddles dry out?

Water does a magical trick when it gets very hot – it becomes invisible! When it bakes in the Sun's heat, it changes into the invisible gas water vapor and floats away in the air.

? What is steam?

When water vapor hits something cold, it cools and starts to change back from an invisible gas into a liquid. We can see steam because it's made up of masses of tiny droplets of liquid water.

❓ *Where does ice come from?*

Ice is what happens when water gets very, very cold – it freezes into a solid. Most materials will change from a liquid into a gas if they get hot enough, and from a liquid into a solid if they get cold enough.

❓ *Why do balloons get bigger?*

One reason balloons get bigger is because you're blowing lots of air into them. The other is because they're made of a stretchy material called rubber. But don't forget to tie a knot to hold the air in, or your balloons will shrink again very quickly!

You cannot weigh air.

FALSE. Like everything on Earth, air has weight – 4,000 balloons would weigh the same as a tub of ice cream.

❓*Why do balloons float?*

Things float upward when they're lighter than their surroundings. Air-filled balloons are roughly the same weight as the air around them, which is why they don't float all that well. The best floaters are filled with a gas that's much lighter than air. It's called helium, and it's used in airships as well as in party balloons.

Most fish use balloons to help them float.

TRUE. Most fish have a gas-filled bag called a swim bladder inside them, which helps them float.

❓ *Why do rubber ducks float in the bathtub?*

Air is lighter than water, and one reason a rubber duck floats is because it's stuffed full of air. The water helps, too, because it pushes up on the duck. This upward push is called upthrust.

❓ *Why does the water level rise when I get in the tub?*

When you get in the bathtub, your body pushes the water out of the way. The only place the water can go is up, so the water level rises.

? *Why does the soap sink?*

Things will float in water only if they are lighter than the amount of water they push aside. If they are heavier, the water's upthrust isn't strong enough to hold them up. A cake of soap will sink if it's heavier than the amount of water it pushes aside.

? *Where does sugar go in hot drinks?*

Sugar doesn't just vanish in hot drinks, it does the same trick in cold ones. It doesn't completely disappear, though – you can taste it's there. You can't see the sugar, because it spreads completely into the water. We call this dissolving.

? *Why do fizzy drinks have bubbles?*

The bubbles in fizzy drinks are the gas carbon dioxide. You can't see them when the top is on the bottle because the carbon dioxide is dissolved in the water.

Lots of carbon dioxide is squashed into the drink, and when you open the bottle, the gas escapes as bubbles.

? Why can't we see in the dark?

We can't see in the dark because we can't see without light. Objects like trees and houses don't give off their own light, even in the daytime. We can only see them because sunlight is bouncing off them into our eyes. This bouncing off is called reflection.

? *Why can I see myself in a mirror?*

When light hits something rough like a blanket, it scatters in all directions – like spilling sugar. But when light hits something smooth like a mirror, it comes straight back – like a ball bouncing off a wall. You see yourself in a mirror because light bounces off your face toward the mirror, and then straight back into your eyes.

Sunlight

Raindrop

Light spreads into colors.

? Is light white?

Light may look white sometimes, but it's really a mixture of all the colors of the rainbow – red, orange, yellow, green, blue, indigo (violet-blue), violet.

? Why do rainbows happen?

Rainbows happen when sunlight passes through water drops. The water drops make white light spread into all its colors, and we see a rainbow.

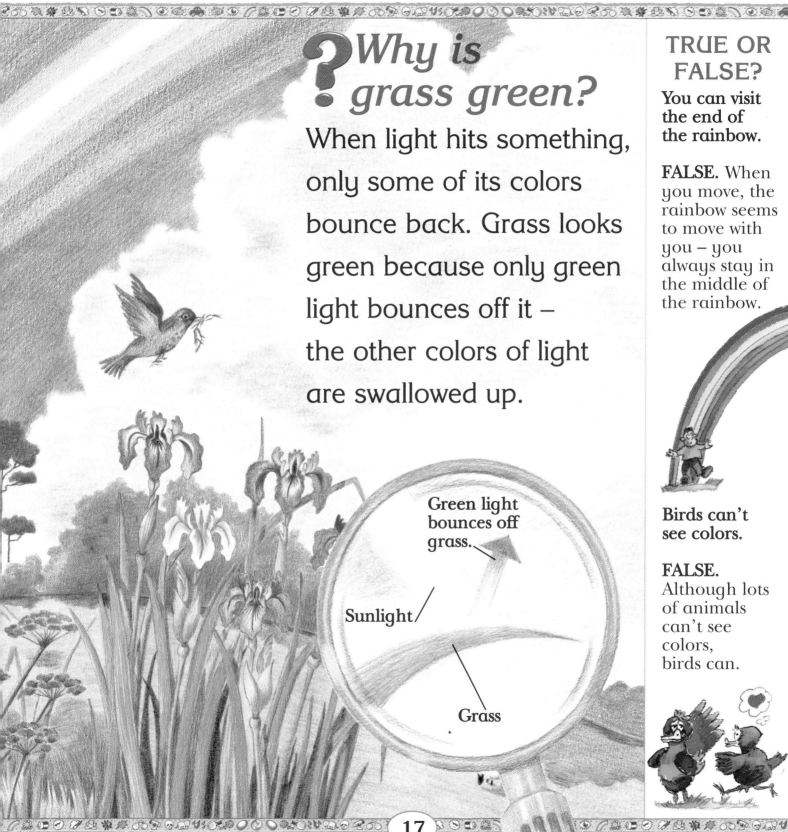

?Why is grass green?

When light hits something, only some of its colors bounce back. Grass looks green because only green light bounces off it – the other colors of light are swallowed up.

Green light bounces off grass.

Sunlight

Grass

? Why does opening the curtains make it light?

Light can pass through some materials, such as window glass, but not others. When materials let light through, we call them transparent.

? Where do shadows come from?

Your body isn't transparent, so it blocks the light and makes the dark patch we call a shadow form. You can test this out on a sunny day – to see your shadow, stand with your back to the Sun.

❓ Why does drawing the curtains make it dark?

When things don't let light through, we call them opaque. If curtains are made of thick, heavy cloth, they can be opaque enough to block light and make rooms dark, even during the day.

Transparent

Opaque

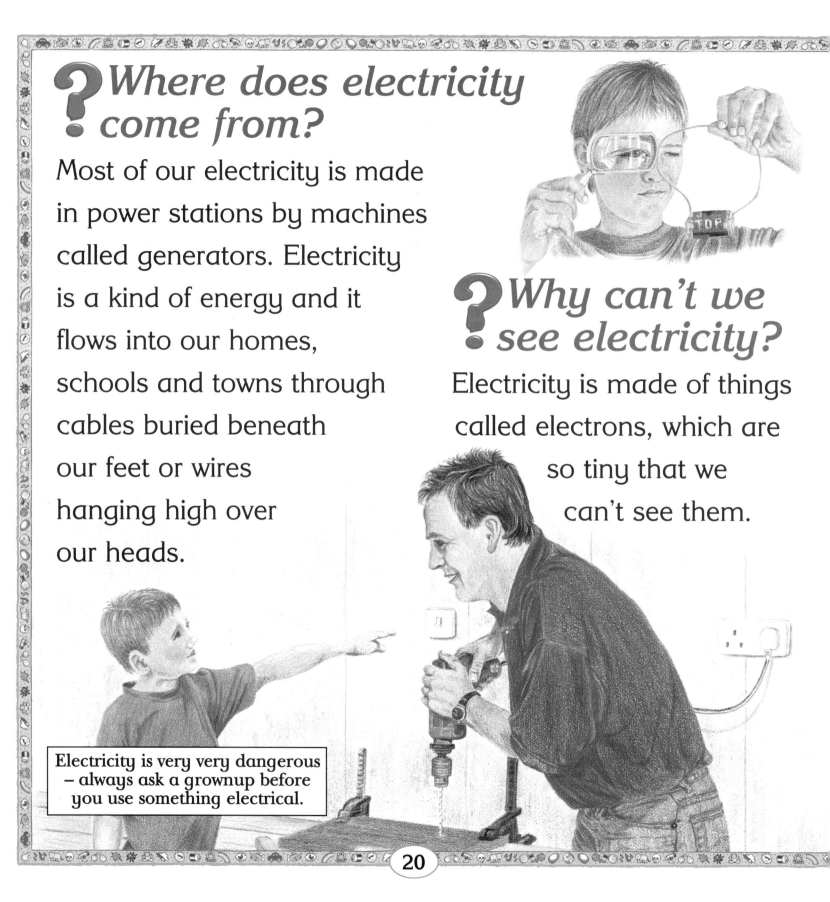

❓ Where does electricity come from?

Most of our electricity is made in power stations by machines called generators. Electricity is a kind of energy and it flows into our homes, schools and towns through cables buried beneath our feet or wires hanging high over our heads.

Electricity is very very dangerous – always ask a grownup before you use something electrical.

❓ Why can't we see electricity?

Electricity is made of things called electrons, which are so tiny that we can't see them.

? How can I make electricity?

? You can make a safe kind of electricity by rubbing a balloon against a nylon sweater. It's called static electricity and it has pulling power – test this out by sticking the balloon on a wall.

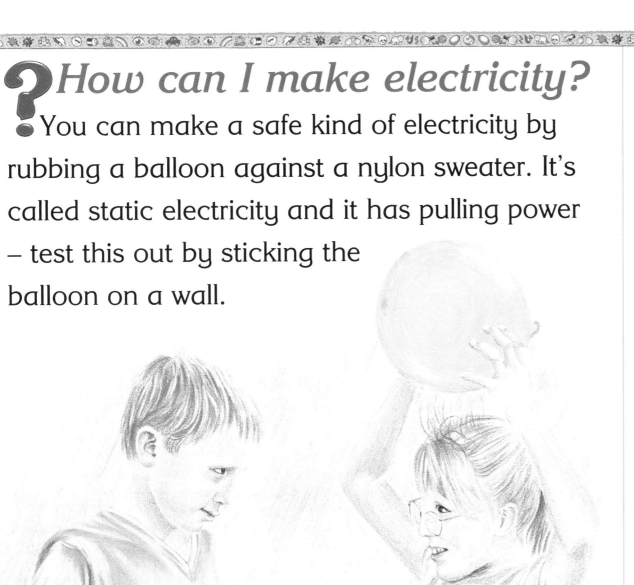

?Why do things stop working when you switch them off?

Electricity only works when it can flow all the way around a loop called a circuit. Turning off a switch breaks the circuit, stopping the flow and turning electrical things like lights off. Turning a switch on joins the circuit and makes them work again.

Ask a grownup to help you make this simple switch and circuit.

Thumbtack

Paper clips act as a switch.

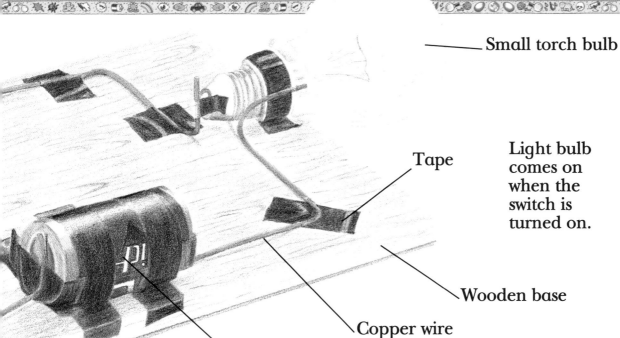

———— Small torch bulb

Tape

Light bulb comes on when the switch is turned on.

Wooden base

Copper wire

1.5 volt battery

❓ *How do batteries make electricity?*

There are metals and other special chemicals inside a battery, which can change to make electricity. The chemicals are dangerous, though, so never open a battery to look at them.

?How can I see sound?

Sound is a kind of energy which happens when something vibrates, or shakes, and makes the air around it vibrate as well. The vibrations travel through the air into your ears, and you hear sounds. You can see sound energy if you sprinkle sugar on a drum and then hit it with a stick. The vibrations will make the sugar shake up and down.

❓ *How do sounds travel along telephone wires?*

Telephones have a microphone in them which changes sound energy into electricity. The electricity flows through wires to another telephone, where a small speaker changes the electricity back into sound energy.

❓Do magnets have glue in them?

No, magnets work because they have an invisible force called magnetism. Most magnets are made of iron or steel, and their magnetism pulls objects made of iron or steel toward them.

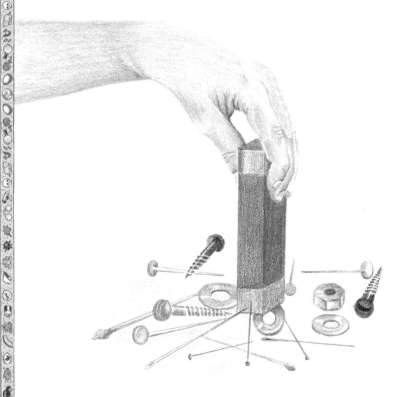

❓How do magnets push and pull?

The two ends of a magnet are called its north and south poles. If you have two magnets, the north pole of one will attract (pull) the south pole of the other toward it. Two north poles or two south poles will repel (push) each other away.

? *How do magnets help explorers?*

Magnets are used in compasses because if a magnet can move freely, its north pole will always swing around to point towards the Earth's North Pole. You can test this out by hanging a bar magnet on a piece of string.

Magnet lines up with north.

NORTH

? Why are slides slippery?

Friction is a slowing force which happens when two surfaces rub against each other. Rough surfaces create stronger friction than smooth ones do, which is why slides are given smooth slippery surfaces. Can you imagine how difficult it would be to slide down a rough concrete ramp?

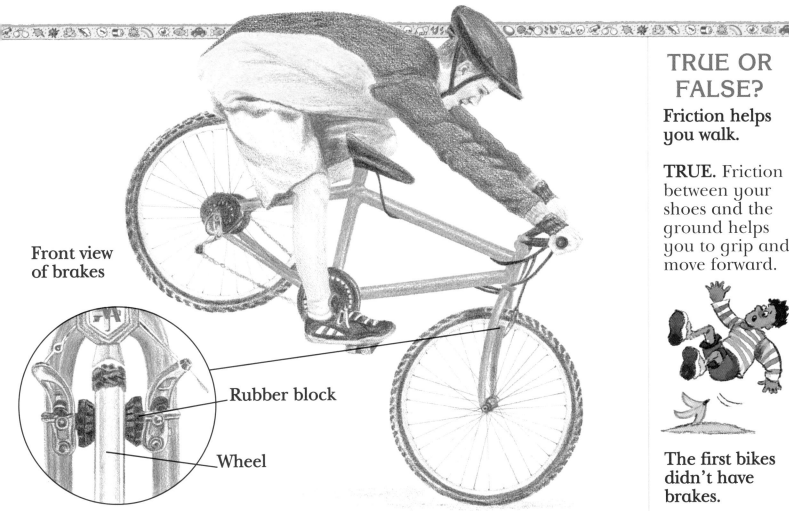

Front view
of brakes

Rubber block

Wheel

❓ *Why do bikes have brakes?*

Brakes help a bike to stop, of course – but do you know why? It's because brakes use friction. When you squeeze the brakes, rubber blocks press against the wheels. The friction between the blocks and the wheels slows your bike down.

Friction helps you walk.

TRUE. Friction between your shoes and the ground helps you to grip and move forward.

The first bikes didn't have brakes.

TRUE. When the earliest bicycles were made in the 1790s, they didn't have brakes or pedals.

❓ Why do I fall over?

You might start to fall because you trip, but it's the invisible force of gravity that makes you end up on the ground. Gravity is a real downer – it's what tugs everything on Earth toward the ground and stops things like balls from flying off into Space.

How fast do skydivers fall?

When skydivers jump out of an airplane they drop toward the ground at about 120 mph. Opening a parachute slows the skydiver down to about 12 mph – but that's still a lot faster than you can run!

What makes things heavy?

Gravity does! Weight is the effect of gravity on an object's mass – the amount of stuff it's made of. The more mass something has, the more gravity tugs it down and the heavier it is.

Index